It's all about ...

VIOLENT
VOLCANOES

KINGFISHER

NEW YORK

KINGFISHER
LONDON & NEW YORK

Copyright © Macmillan Publishers International Ltd 2016
Published in the United States by Kingfisher,
175 Fifth Ave., New York, NY 10010
Kingfisher is an imprint of Macmillan Children's Books, London
All rights reserved.

Distributed in the U.S. and Canada by Macmillan,
175 Fifth Ave., New York, NY 10010

Library of Congress Cataloging-in-Publication data
has been applied for.

Series editor: Sarah Snashall
Series design: Little Red Ant
Adapted from an original text by Claire Llewellyn, Thea Feldman

ISBN 978-0-7534-7268-2

Kingfisher books are available for special promotions
and premiums. For details contact: Special Markets
Department, Macmillan, 175 Fifth Ave.,
New York, NY 10010.

For more information, please visit
www.kingfisherbooks.com

Printed in China

9 8 7 6 5 4 3 2

2TR/0216/WKT/UG/128MA

Picture credits
The Publisher would like to thank the following for permission to reproduce their material.
Top = t; Bottom = b; Center = c; Left = l; Right = r
Cover Shutterstock/Rainer Albiez; Back Cover Shutterstock/James Jones Jr.; Pages
2–3 Shutterstock/Gardar Olafsson; 4–5 Shutterstock/Rainer Albiez; 6–7 Shutterstock/G Seeger;
7 Corbis/Gary Braasch; 8–9 Kingfisher artbank; 10 Shutterstock/Catmando; 11 Kingfisher
Artbank; 12–13 Shutterstock/Robert Crow; 13 Shutterstock/Kemal Taner; 14 Kingfisher
Artbank; 15, 16–17 Shutterstock/Amy Nichole Harris; 17 Shutterstock/khd; 18 Shutterstock/
Gardar Olafsson; 19t Shutterstock/Graeme Shannon; 19b Shutterstock/Andyz;
20–21b Kingfisher Artbank; 20–21 Shutterstock/Andreas Koeberl; 22 SPL/Anakaopress;
23 SPL/Jeremy Bishop; 24–25 Shutterstock/zschnepf; 25 Shutterstock/nikolpetr;
26–27 Shutterstock/Robert Hoetink; 27 Shutterstock/KPG Payless2; 28 NASA/JPL; 29 NASA/
ESA; 30–31 Shutterstock/Gardar Olafsson; 32 Shutterstock/Robert Crow.
Cards: Front: tl Shutterstock/Valeriy Poltorak; bl Shutterstock/Sailorr; tr Shutterstock/
jukurae; br Shutterstock/Byelikova Oksana; Back: tl Shutterstock/saraporn; bl Shutterstock/
Albert Barr; tr Shutterstock/Little_Desire; br Corbis/Alberto Garcia.

Front cover: Mount Stromboli erupts off the coast of Sicily, Italy.

CONTENTS

Fireworks!

Most of the time a volcano looks like any other mountain, but every so often it throws out gas, ash, and burning rock. This is called an eruption.

The biggest eruptions are like firework displays. There is a lot of noise, and red-hot rock shoots out of the volcano's peak.

FACT...

The word "volcano" comes from the name Vulcan. Vulcan was the Roman god of fire.

Sudden danger

In the spring of 1980, life was quiet on Mount St. Helens. Snow and ice covered the top of the mountain. Thick forests grew across its slopes.

On May 18, Mount St. Helens suddenly erupted.

There was a huge blast and great clouds of smoke shot out of its peak. The snow and ice melted and water gushed down the hillside.

The ash cloud rose 15 mi. (24km) into the atmosphere.

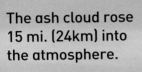

SPOTLIGHT: Mount St. Helens

Height:	7380 ft. (2250m)
Famous for:	major eruption May 18, 1980
Last erupted:	July 10, 2010
Status:	active

Blasted away

During the eruption, part of the peak of Mount St. Helens was blown away and a hole was blasted in its side. The snow and ice disappeared.

FACT...

The sound of the eruption could be heard hundreds of miles away.

The forests were knocked down. Many animals were killed and 57 people died. An erupting volcano is one of the most powerful things on Earth.

Mount St. Helens was 1300 feet (400 meters) shorter after the eruption.

Inside a volcano

Inside a volcano there is a deep hole.
This hole goes down inside Earth to
the hot, melted rock called magma.
Sometimes the magma rises up the hole
and flows out of the volcano as lava.

FACT ...

**Every day about 20 volcanoes erupt
in the world.**

The lava pours downhill, cools, and hardens. Every time the volcano erupts, a new layer of lava pours out. The layers build up and form a cone.

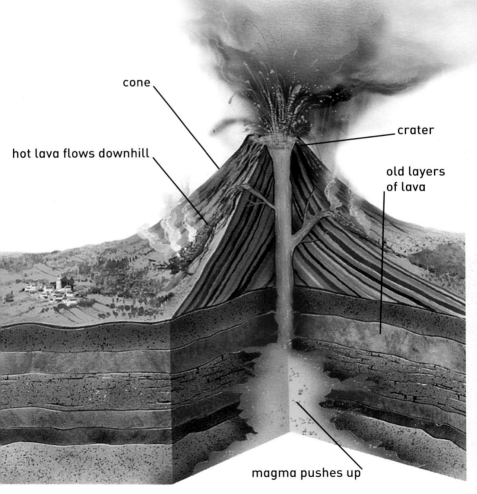

cone

crater

hot lava flows downhill

old layers of lava

magma pushes up

Run for your life!

Each volcanic eruption is different. Sometimes, lava seeps out slowly and gas comes out in puffs.

FACT ...

The most dangerous part of a volcanic eruption is not the lava but the ground-level cloud of superheated ash, rock, and gas that can travel at 430 mph (700km/h).

Sometimes an eruption is like a bomb going off! Farms, villages, and roads are destroyed by shooting rocks, fast-moving hot ash, and burning lava.

SPOTLIGHT: Mount Merapi, Java, Indonesia

Height:	9600 ft. (2930m)
Famous for:	major eruption 2010
Last erupted:	March to April 2014
Status:	active

This house in Sicily has been buried in lava.

Pompeii

One afternoon in August 79CE the people of Pompeii, in Italy, heard a loud bang. They looked up and saw clouds of ash shooting out of the top of nearby Mount Vesuvius.

People fled as Mount Vesuvius erupted.

SPOTLIGHT: Mount Vesuvius, Italy

Height:	4203 ft. (1281m)
Famous for:	destroying Pompeii, 79ce
Last eruption:	1944
Status:	active

Soon the air was filled with falling rocks, gas, and ash. Within hours Pompeii was buried under ash and lava. Thousands of people and animals died.

The ruins of Pompeii have now been uncovered.

The hidden town

When the ash and lava hardened, Pompeii was buried under a layer of rock 16 feet (5 meters) thick. It lay hidden for 1500 years until it was found by some people digging a well. Soon people found streets, stores, and houses buried under the rock.

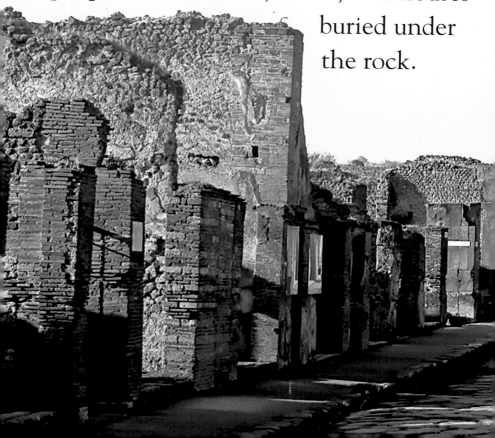

Bronze statues, colorful paintings, and everyday items were found in Pompeii.

FACT ...

The nearby Roman cities of Herculaneum and Stabiae were also buried in the ash from Vesuvius.

Beautiful paintings such as this one were found on the walls of some houses in Pompeii.

Active, dormant, or extinct?

Volcanoes can be sorted into three groups: active, dormant, and extinct.

Active volcanoes erupt fairly often.

FACT ...

Earth has more than 1500 active volcanoes.

This volcano in Iceland erupted in 2010.

Dormant volcanoes have not erupted for a very long time, but might erupt again.

Mount Kilimanjaro is a dormant volcano in Africa.

Extinct volcanoes are very old and will never erupt again.

Diamond Head is an extinct volcano in Hawaii.

Undersea volcanoes

There are around 1000 volcanoes under the ocean. Over a long time they become islands.

1. Lava pours out of a hole in the ocean floor.

2. The lava cools and hardens into rock.

The tallest mountain on Earth is an undersea volcano called Mauna Kea. It's 33,500 feet (10,200 meters) tall (starting at the ocean floor)—that's 4430 feet (1350 meters) taller than Mount Everest, the highest mountain on land!

More than half of Mauna Kea is underwater.

SPOTLIGHT: Mauna Kea, Hawaii

Height:	13,802 ft. (4207m) above ocean
Famous for:	volcano rises from ocean floor
Last erupted:	4600 years ago
Status:	dormant

3. Each time the volcano erupts it grows taller.

A dangerous job

Scientists study volcanoes and try to predict when they will erupt. They measure the volcano's size to see if magma under the ground is making it swell. They check to see if the ground is getting hotter.

Volcano experts crawl into craters to collect rock, ash, and gas. They wear special heatproof clothes, but it is still dangerous work. If scientists think a volcano will erupt, they can move local people away from the danger.

Volcano experts have an exciting but dangerous job.

Visit a volcano!

Most volcanoes are safe to visit. If you walk to the top, you can look down into the crater. You may even smell the gases from inside Earth. (They smell like rotten cabbages and eggs!)

Crater Lake, Oregon, is an extinct volcano. It is perfect for sailing and swimming.

Walkers climb a volcano in Japan.

SPOTLIGHT: Sakurajima, Japan

Height:	3664 ft. (1117m)
Famous for:	extremely active volcano
Last erupted:	continually erupting
Status:	active and dangerous

Volcanic riches

Surprisingly, many people choose to live on or near an active volcano. Some of these people are farmers because the soil on a volcano is very rich in minerals.

The water in this lake in Iceland is heated by volcanic rocks.

In other places, people live near volcanoes because the heat from volcanoes is free—and it never runs out. People use this heat to warm their buildings.

These bananas are growing using the heat from a volcano.

FACT...

Around 500 million people in the world live on or near an active volcano.

Volcanoes in space

You will find volcanoes all over
our planet. If you could
travel into space, you
would find them on
other planets, too.

Io (a moon of Jupiter.) The dots all over
its surface are very big, active volcanoes.
A volcano is erupting next to the orange area.

Height:	14 mi. (22km)
Famous for:	largest volcano in solar system
Last erupted:	50 to 25 million years ago
Status:	dormant

Olympus Mons is a volcano on Mars. It is 14 miles (22 kilometers) high—about three times higher than Mount Everest!

GLOSSARY

ash The soft, gray dust that is left after a fire.

blast A big bang or explosion.

bronze A red-brown metal.

cone The rocky, steep-sided shape of a volcano.

crater The bowl-like hole at the top of a volcano.

dormant As if asleep; inactive at the moment but may erupt again.

erupt To throw out lava, ash, and gas.

eruption When a volcano throws out hot rock and gases.

experts People who know a lot about a subject.

extinct Has stopped erupting forever.

gas A very light, shapeless substance that is not solid or runny. Air is made of gases.

lava The hot, melted rock that comes out of a volcano.

magma The hot, melted rock inside Earth.

mineral A useful type of rock found in the ground.

ocean floor The bottom of the ocean.

peak The pointed top of a mountain.

predict To say what will happen in the future.

seep To flow slowly.

swell To become bigger all over.

INDEX